Explore and Draw

MONSTER TRUCKS

Ann Becker

ROURKE PUBLISHING

www.rourkepublishing.com

www.rourkepublishing.com

Editor: Penny Dowdy
Art Direction: Tarang Saggar (Q2AMedia)
Designer: Divij Singh (Q2AMedia)
Picture researcher: Mariea Janet (Q2AMedia)
Picture credits:
t=top b=bottom c=centre l=left r=right

Cover: Michael Stokes/Shutterstock.
Insides: P6 : BIGFOOT 4x4 Inc, P7 : BIGFOOT 4x4 Inc, P15: BIGFOOT 4x4 Inc,
P10 : TheMonsterBlog, P11 : TheMonsterBlog, P14 : TheMonsterBlog , P15 : TheMonsterBlog,
P18 : TheMonsterBlog. Border Images: Up images/Shutterstock, Ali Mazraie Shadi/Shutterstock, EcoPrint/Shutterstock,
Mechanik/Shutterstock, Mechanik/Shutterstock, Blaz Kure/Shutterstock, sabri deniz kizil/Shutterstock, Jose AS Reyes/Shutterstock,
Sergei Butorin/Shutterstock, renkshot/Shutterstock, Rob Wilson/Shutterstock, afaizal/Shutterstock, bioraven/Shutterstock,
hfng/Shutterstock, Anastasios Kandris/Shutterstock, Shutterstock, Péter Gudella/Shutterstock.
Q2AMedia Art Bank: Cover Page, Title Page, P4-5, P8-9, P12-13, P16-17, P20-21.

Library of Congress Cataloging-in-Publication Data

Becker, Ann, 1965 Oct. 6-
Monster trucks : explore and draw / Ann Becker.
p. cm. – (Explore and draw)
Includes index.
ISBN 978-1-60694-354-0 (hard cover)
ISBN 978-1-60694-838-5 (soft cover)
1. Trucks in art–Juvenile literature. 2. Monster trucks–Juvenile literature.
3. Drawing–Technique–Juvenile literature. I. Title. II. Title: Explore and draw.
NC825.T76B43 2009
743'.896292232–dc22
2009021616

Printed by: Corporate Graphics, Inc
Manufactured in: North Mankato, Minnesota, USA
050511
050211LP-A

www.rourkepublishing.com - rourke@rourkepublishing.com
Post Office Box 643328 Vero Beach, Florida 32964

Contents

Technique

Before you start drawing monster trucks, let's talk about **contrast**. Contrast is making different areas of your drawing light or dark.

1

The monster truck is close up, so it is drawn with high contrast. Notice how different the light and dark areas are. When drawing objects that are close up, you should use strong contrast. The light parts are very light and the dark parts are very dark.

2

The second monster is far away, so it is drawn with less contrast. Notice that the dark and light areas are not as different. Objects that are far away have less contrast, so the difference in dark and light items is less.

Monster Truck History

Bob Chandler is the father of monster trucks. He turned his interest in driving off road into a new sport.

Four-by-Fours

In most cars, the engine either makes the front or rear wheels move, and the other two wheels just roll along. In a **4x4**, the engine moves all four wheels. This gives the vehicle better control on the ground.

The original Big Foot looks tame compared to the monster trucks today!

Here Comes Big Foot

Chandler loved driving 4x4 trucks so much, he built one of his own. He installed large tractor wheels, lights, and bumpers. The truck was so unusual, it got attention everywhere it went.

With so many fans, Chandler wanted to enter the truck in a custom car show. But because it was not a car, Big Foot was not allowed. Finally, in 1979, Big Foot was invited to a show in Denver, and then to other events across the country.

Today Bob Chandler has a fleet of Big Foot trucks that compete in rallies around the country.

Monster Truck Rallies

Big Foot performed at many tractor pulls, where Chandler would crush cars and do other stunts. Soon, more fans were showing up to see Chandler and Big Foot than the tractor pulls! Chandler organized events that just featured monster trucks, and the sport was born.

Draw Big Foot

Today's Big Foot has much larger wheels and a different frame than the original.

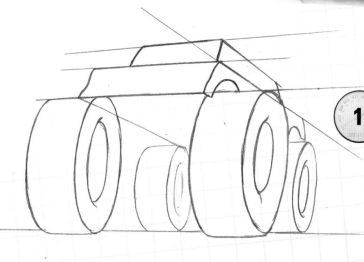

1 Use light pencil marks to sketch the basic shape of the truck.

2 Add the simple lines that create the treads on the tires and details on the body of the truck.

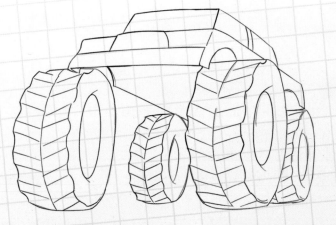

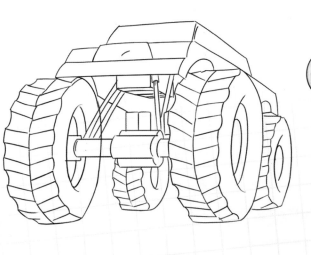

3 There are many shapes and lines under the truck, too.

4 Remember that the front of the truck is close, so it would have high contrast. The back of the truck is farther away, so the contrast is lower.

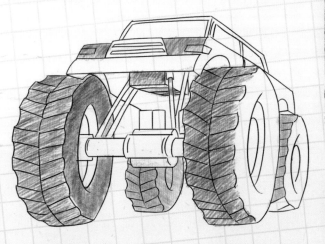

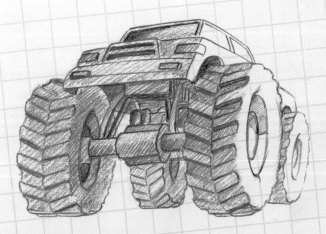

5 Finish shading Big Foot to complete your drawing.

Obstacle Courses

At a monster truck rally, you will see a variety of events. One event is an **obstacle** course.

Get Over It

On an obstacle course, objects are placed in the way of the drivers. If you were a normal driver, you would drive around obstacles. But at a monster truck rally, the audience wants to see the trucks go over the obstacles. Drivers may jump their trucks off of ramps and into the air. They also may just drive over the obstacles, crushing them as they do!

This truck takes a hard landing after jumping off a ramp.

The Course

The shape of the track depends on where the rally is held. Usually, an outdoor course is set up as a straight line, called a **drag strip**. The car that makes it to the end of the strip fastest gets the most points. Trucks can earn extra points by jumping ramps and crushing obstacles.

Indoor tracks are short and rectangular. The trucks race around the track a number of times, jumping ramps and crushing obstacles. Again, they earn points with their stunts and speed.

Junk Cars

One key part of an obstacle course are the junk cars. They are lined up and stacked on the course. Watching a truck pounce onto a pile of cars or drive over them is an audience favorite.

A driver can win as much as $100,000 by winning a major race.

Draw Grave Digger

Grave Digger's creator has made 29 versions of the truck to race!

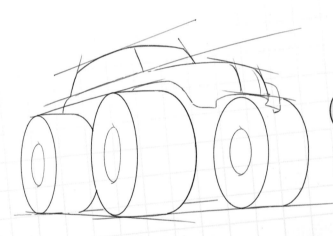

1 Look at the simple outline of the truck and its wheels.

2 Add the treads to all four tires.

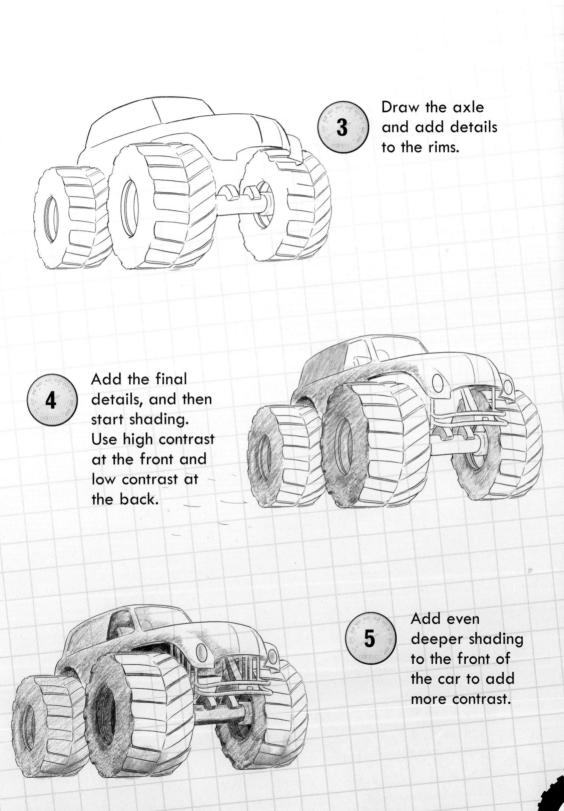

3 Draw the axle and add details to the rims.

4 Add the final details, and then start shading. Use high contrast at the front and low contrast at the back.

5 Add even deeper shading to the front of the car to add more contrast.

Freestyle

Another event at a monster truck rally is the **freestyle**. Each driver has 60 seconds to do as many tricks as possible.

More Junk

Just like the obstacle course, the freestyle uses junk cars. A driver climbs over piles of trucks, and jumps off of ramps to fly over cars. If the truck misses the jump and lands on the cars, that's exciting, too!

This truck, named Bounty Hunter, is a champion of freestyle competitions.

The freestyle competition lets drivers perform their most amazing tricks.

Tire Tricks

During the freestyle **competition**, drivers will spin and tip the trucks for points, too. A driver will do **donuts**, where he drives in tight circles. The faster he goes, the more likely that he loses control of the truck or that it tips over. Donuts also kick up a lot of dust and dirt. In a **wheelie**, the driver will put the truck on its back two wheels. The longer the truck stays on two wheels, the more points the driver earns. Of course, if the driver tips the wheelie too far back, the truck will flip over!

The Big Jump

One of the most exciting parts of the freestyle competition is the big jump. The course is set up with a huge object, such as a bus, a trailer, or even a mobile home! Then the driver takes the ramp as fast as he can. At this high speed, the truck jumps. These tricks earn a lot of points!

Draw a Wheelie

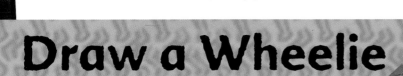

Drivers perform a lot of wheelies at a Monster Truck Rally.

1 A truck doing a wheelie is at an angle. Use the guide lines to help with that.

2 Draw the bed of the truck and the treads of the tires.

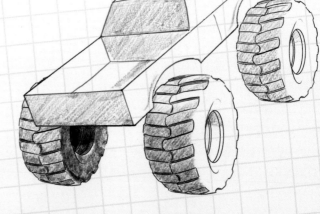

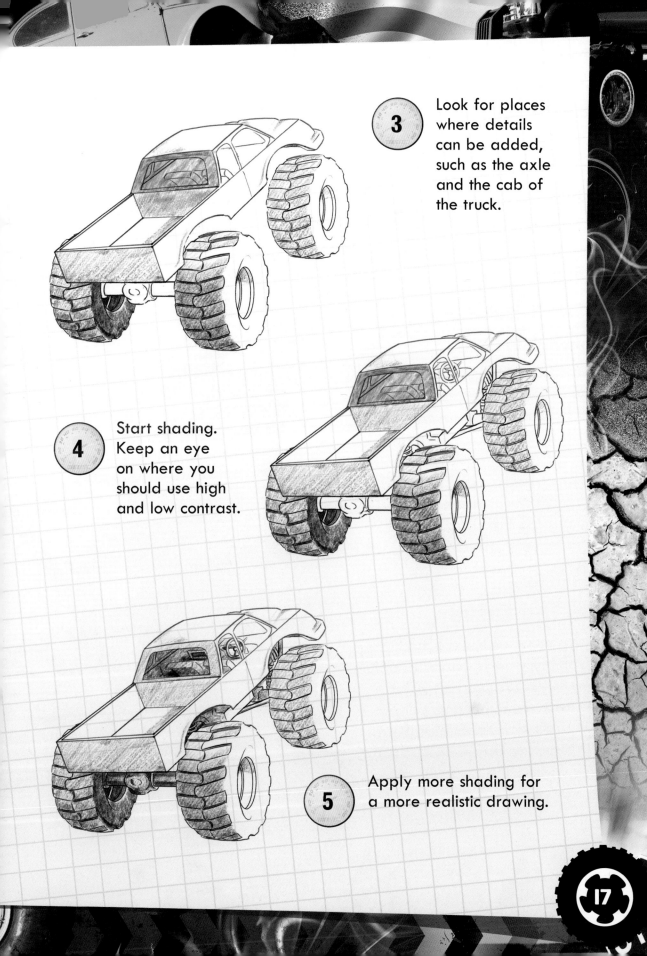

3 Look for places where details can be added, such as the axle and the cab of the truck.

4 Start shading. Keep an eye on where you should use high and low contrast.

5 Apply more shading for a more realistic drawing.

Monster Truck Musts

Monster truck competitions are thrilling for the audience, but the tricks can be dangerous for the drivers.

In the Truck

A truck that a driver competes with is not your ordinary pick-up. The truck is built to stand up to poundings every time it jumps or crashes. The frame of the truck is **reinforced**. The back and cab have roll bars. This keeps the truck from crushing the driver if it flips or rolls over.

On the Driver

The driver wears a lot of protective gear, too. Helmets and neck braces keep the driver safe if he is knocked around the cab. The uniform he wears is **flame-retardant**. This means the clothing does not burn easily if the truck catches fire.

Monster truck drivers wear clothing and gear that protect them from injury.

At the Track

Rules at the racetrack help keep everyone safe. Before a driver can compete, he must get a special license to show he knows how to safely race the truck. Everyone on the track follows other safety rules. For example, when the trucks are racing, people are not allowed on the track.

The truck has safety equipment, too, so that drivers can stay safe through crashes and fires.

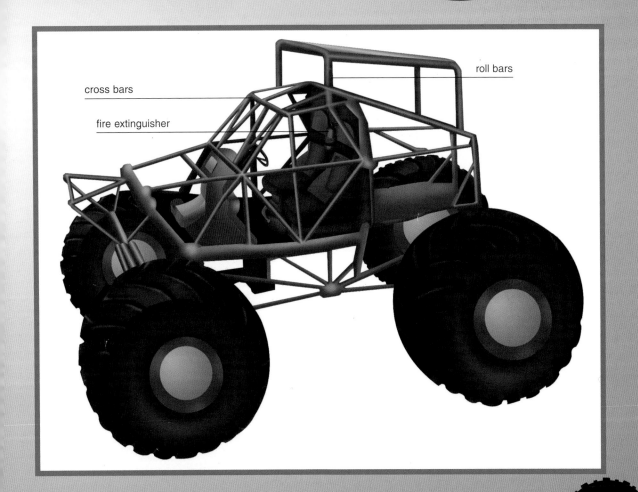

roll bars

cross bars

fire extinguisher

Draw the Frame

The frame is under the truck's skin. The strong steel tubes keep the driver safe in a crash.

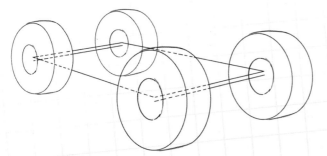

1 Start with the base of the chassis and the wheels.

2 Bars run through the base of the chassis to hold the weight of the truck.

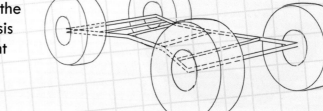

3 Add more bars to the frame, and draw the treads on the tires.

4 Add the last bars to the frame, and start shading with high and low contrast.

5 Shade and blend a bit more to finish your drawing.

Glossary

4x4 (FOR-bye-for): a vehicle with an engine that powers all four wheels

competition (kom-puh-TISH-uhn): a contest or race

contrast (KON-trast): to show the difference between dark and light

donuts (DOH-nuts): driving in a tight circle

drag strip (DRAG STRIP): a long, straight race track

flame-retardant (FLAYM ri-TARD-ent): something that resists burning

freestyle (FREE-stile): a competition with no set way to perform

obstacle (OB-stuh-kuhl): something in the way of a moving object

reinforced (ree-in-FORSST): strengthened

wheelie (WEEL-ee): driving on rear wheels only

Index

Websites

http://www.bigfoot4x4.com/
The website for the original monster truck and the Big Foot racing team.

http://www.monsterjamonline.com/
The official website for Monster Jam, which features news, results, photos, videos, and more.

http://www.monstertruckracing.com/
Photos of monster trucks in action are featured on this website.

drawsketch.about.com/od/kidsdrawingpages/Kids_Pages_Childrens
A website which provides lists on how to draw a variety of things.

http://www.monstertrucks.net/directory.asp?category=3
Directory of websites of monster trucks and their drivers

http://www.monsternationals.com/
The official website for a family-oriented truck organization.

About the Author
Ann Becker is an avid reader. Ann likes to read books, magazines, and even Internet articles. She hopes that someday she will get to go on a game show and put all of that reading to good use!

About the Illustrator
Maria Menon has been illustrating children's books for almost a decade. She loves making illustrations of animals, especially dragons and dinosaurs. She is fond of pets and has two dogs named Spot and Lara. When she is not busy illustrating, Maria spends her time watching animated movies.